GENETICS

ANIMAL CELLS

by Mason Anders

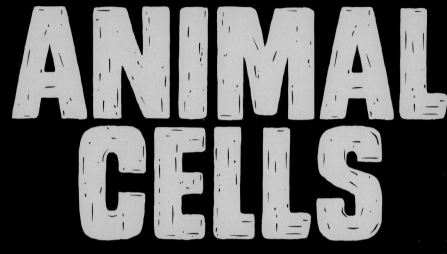

CAPSTONE PRESS

a capstone imprint

Fact Finders Books are published by Capstone Press,
1710 Roe Crest Drive, North Mankato, Minnesota 56003
www.mycapstone.com

Library of Congress Cataloging-in-Publication Data
Names: Anders, Mason, author.
Title: Animal cells / by Mason Anders.
Description: North Mankato, Minnesota : Capstone Press, [2017] | Series: Fact finders. Genetics |
   Includes bibliographical references and index.
Identifiers: LCCN 2016055791
   ISBN 978-1-5157-7259-0 (library binding)
   ISBN 978-1-5157-7263-7 (paperback)
   ISBN 978-1-5157-7267-5 (ebook pdf)
Subjects: LCSH: Cell physiology—Juvenile literature. | Cells—Juvenile literature.
Classification: LCC QH631 .A53 2017 | DDC 571.6/3—dc23
LC record available at https://lccn.loc.gov/2016055791

Editorial Credits
Editor: Nikki Potts
Designer: Philippa Jenkins
Media Researcher: Morgan Walters and Jo Miller
Production Specialist: Katy LaVigne

Photo Credits
Alamy: Universal Images Group North America LLC, 16; ScienceSource: Dr. Cecil H. Fox, 11, Science Picture Co, 7; Shutterstock: Alila Medical Media, 29, Andrii Muzyka, 26, BlueRingMedia, 24, Crevis, 15, decade3d - anatomyonline, 22, Denis Kuvaev, 21, Designua, 10, 12, 13, 19, 20, Kateryna Kon, cover (inset), 1, Michael Rosskothen, 5, Mopic, 6, panda3800, 3, photowind, 4, royaltystockphoto.com, 23 (top), sciencepics, 9, Shilova Ekaterina, 23, (bottom), special for you, throughout, (background), Tefi, 17, 27, Volodymyr Krasyuk, cover (leopard)

Printed and bound in China.
004640

TABLE OF CONTENTS

CHAPTER 1

What Is an Animal Cell?

A butterfly wing. A fish scale. A human's beating heart. Each part of every organism is made up of tiny cells. A cell is the smallest unit of life. Most cells are so tiny you need a microscope to see them.

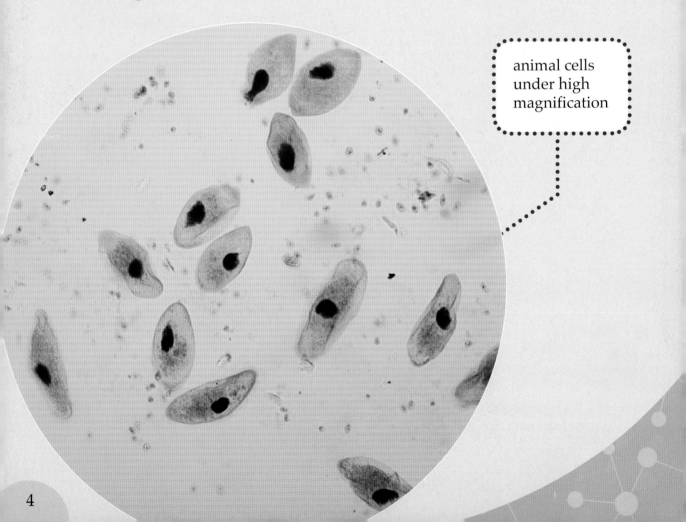

animal cells under high magnification

Blue whales have approximately 100 quadrillion cells.

The bigger the animal, the more cells it has. Some organisms, such as bacteria, are made up of just one cell. A human body is made up of 60 trillion to 100 trillion cells. The blue whale, the largest animal that has ever lived, contains the most cells. It has about 1,000 times as many cells as a human being.

A cell provides the basic structure and function for every living thing. Each animal cell works 24 hours, 7 days a week. It takes in food and gives off waste products. Cell work is responsible for all the life processes that keep animals alive and healthy.

CHAPTER 2

Parts of an Animal Cell

An animal cell has three main parts: the cell membrane, the nucleus, and the cytoplasm.

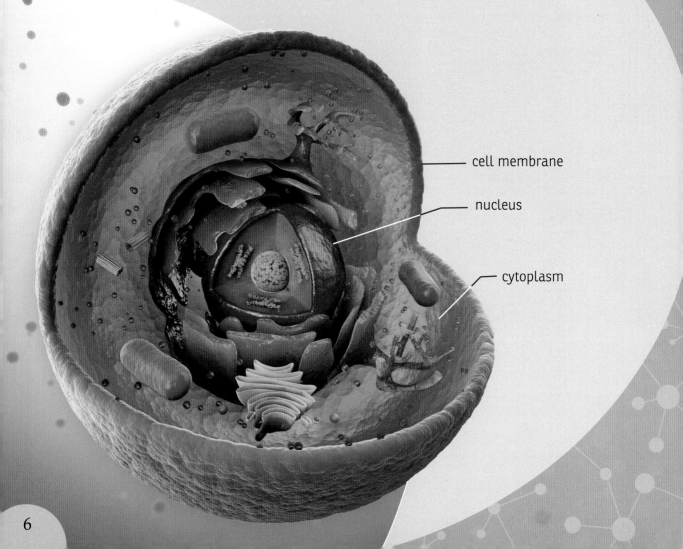

cell membrane

nucleus

cytoplasm

The cell membrane lets substances such as proteins and carbohydrates pass in and out of the cell.

Cell Membrane

A cell membrane acts like the skin of the cell. It holds the cell together. It also acts as the cell's security system. The membrane has tiny openings that allow substances to pass through. The membrane only lets in what the cell needs to live, such as water and food. It only lets out wastes and other chemicals the cell does not need.

Nucleus

The nucleus is the cell's command center. Every part of the cell gets instructions from the nucleus. **Genes** in the nucleus tell the cell what to do. Each gene is a section of a molecule called DNA, which stands for **deoxyribonucleic acid**. DNA is like an instruction manual or a blueprint. It contains a code for all the functions of a cell. DNA determines thousands of characteristics about an animal or person, such as sex, skin color, height, and more. It is what makes each species and each individual animal unique.

The nucleus is surrounded by a nuclear membrane. Tiny pores in the membrane let some substances pass in and out. However, DNA never leaves the nucleus. Information carried by the DNA is coded onto another molecule called **ribonucleic acid**, or RNA. RNA is like a messenger. It can leave the nucleus. RNA carries DNA's instructions into the rest of the cell.

FACT

DNA molecules bundle into **chromosomes**. Each chromosome is made of thousands of genes. Each species has a different number of chromosomes. A human has 46 chromosomes.

gene—tiny unit of a cell that determines the characteristics that an offspring gets from his or her parents

deoxyribonucleic acid (DNA)—the molecule that carries the genes; found inside the nucleus of cells

Each cell nucleus holds a complete set of DNA — the instruction manual for the entire animal. In other words one person's or animal's skin cell and a blood cell both carry the same DNA. In that case, how can those two cells be so different? Each cell is reading just part of the instruction manual. It only follows certain genes in the nucleus.

nucleus

ribonucleic acid (RNA)—the complex molecule produced by living cells and viruses that is responsible for manufacturing the protein in a cell

chromosome—threadlike structure in the nucleus that carries the genes

Cytoplasm

Cytoplasm is a jellylike fluid that surrounds the nucleus. It fills the rest of the cell. Stiff fibers stretch across the cytoplasm. These make up the cell's cytoskeleton. Cells do not have a fixed or rigid structure, like a real skeleton. But the hairlike fibers give shape to the cell and help it move. **Organelles** float inside the cytoplasm.

Monocytes are a type of white blood cell. Blood cells are a type of animal cell.

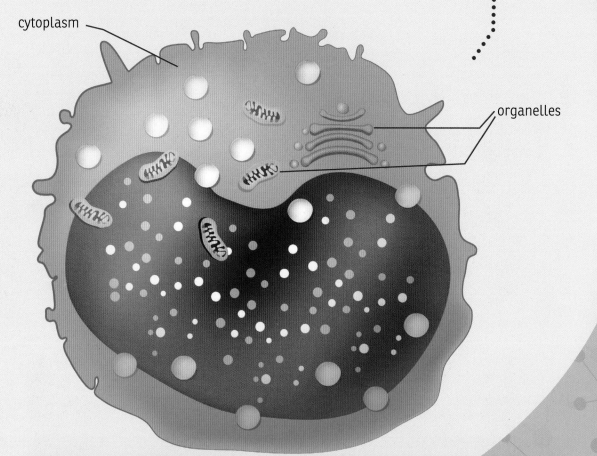

cytoplasm

organelles

organelle—a small structure in a cell that performs a specific function and is surrounded by its own membrane

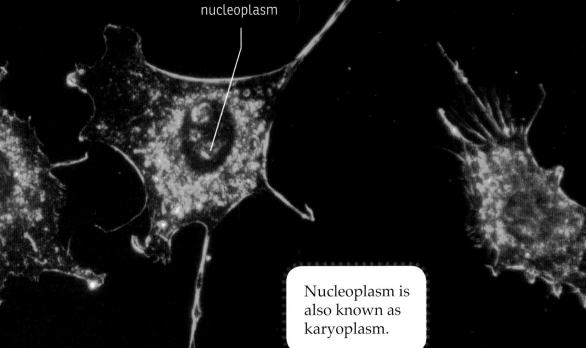

nucleoplasm

Nucleoplasm is also known as karyoplasm.

NUCLEOPLASM

While cytoplasm is the fluid that fills a cell around the nucleus, there is another type of fluid within the nucleus itself. This fluid is called nucleoplasm. It is made of water, molecules, and dissolved ions. It is very sticky.

The nucleoplasm is a suspension fluid — it holds the nucleus and chromosomes. Besides supporting the structure of the nucleus, the nucleoplasm dissolves enzymes and other substances. It also aids in transporting materials that are vital to the cell.

Nucleoplasm is not always present inside the nucleus. When a cell divides, the cell membrane dissolves, and the nucleoplasm is released. After a cell nucleus forms again, nucleoplasm fills the space once again.

CHAPTER 3

Organelles

Each organelle does a specific job. Most animal cells have three main organelles. They are the endoplasmic reticulum, the Golgi apparatus, and the mitochondria. These three organelles do most of the cell's work. Other organelles remove waste and provide storage.

Endoplasmic Reticulum

The endoplasmic reticulum (ER) is where new molecules are made. There are two kinds of ER — smooth and rough. Smooth ER is a series of folded membranes. One of its jobs is to make substances called lipids, also known as fats. These molecules store energy, build cell parts, and send messages.

The surface of rough ER is covered with bumps called ribosomes. Following instructions from DNA, ribosomes help link important molecules called proteins. A cell's proteins affect what it is like and what it can do. Proteins are the building blocks for many things a cell needs.

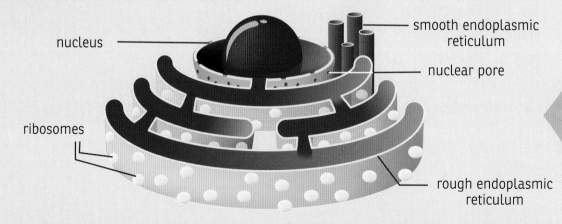

nucleus

ribosomes

smooth endoplasmic reticulum

nuclear pore

rough endoplasmic reticulum

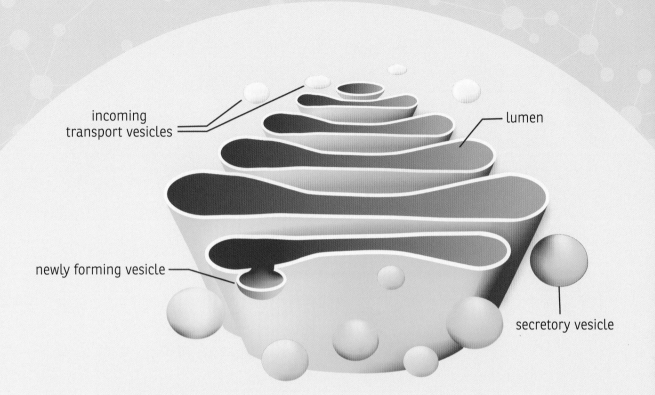

incoming transport vesicles

lumen

newly forming vesicle

secretory vesicle

Golgi Apparatus

Once the ER makes molecules, the Golgi apparatus decides what to do with them. It may keep proteins to be used somewhere within the cell. It may also send the proteins out to be used by other cells.

The Golgi apparatus is the packing and shipping center of the cell. Here important molecules are packaged into membrane-bound pouches. The pouches are sorted depending on where they need to go. Each package has its own address. A chemical tag on the package directs where it should be delivered.

Mitochondria

Mitochondria are the power plants of the cell. Like power plants, they need fuel to work. Mitochondria get their fuel from the food an animal eats. First, the food must be broken down into a form that can enter the cell.

The food an animal eats is first digested. The stomach and intestines break it down into molecules that enter the bloodstream. The most common food molecule is simple sugar, or glucose. The blood then carries glucose to cells everywhere in the body.

The cell membrane lets glucose into the cell. A glucose molecule stores plenty of food energy. However, a cell cannot make use of this energy directly. First, glucose must be converted into another molecule. The mitochondria convert the glucose into a chemical called adenosine triphosphate, or ATP. Cells use ATP to power many cell functions. For example, ATP helps build new proteins, move molecules around the cell, and make more cells.

This process of converting glucose to ATP is called cellular respiration. It is a crucial life process. If cellular respiration stops, an animal will die within minutes.

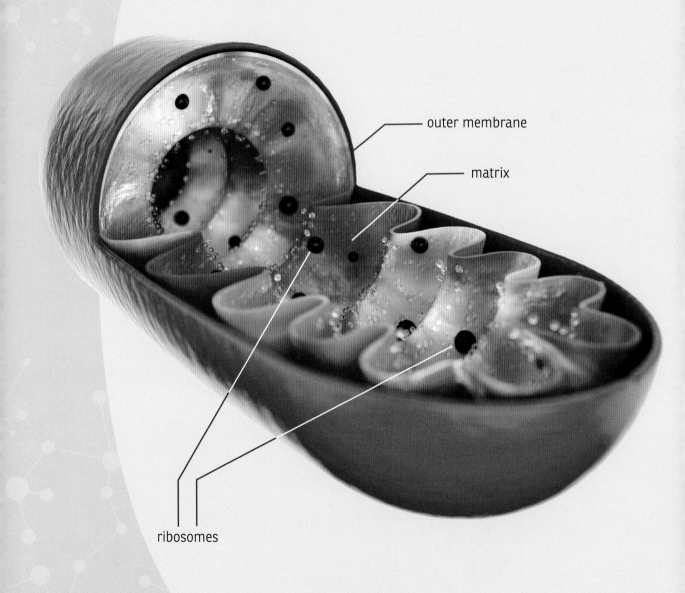

outer membrane

matrix

ribosomes

Other Organelles

Lysosomes form the cell's waste disposal system. These pouches take in and break down unwanted materials from the rest of the cell. They have special chemicals that digest worn-out cell parts, germs, or other cell waste.

Vacuoles are the cell's storage centers. These pouches store water and food, like a sandwich in a plastic bag.

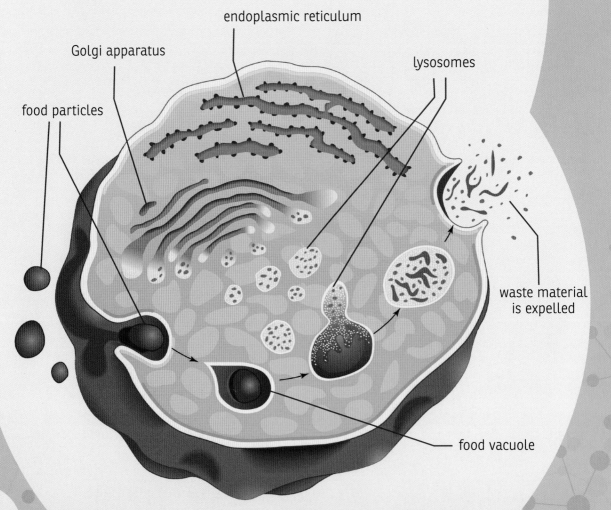

endoplasmic reticulum

Golgi apparatus

lysosomes

food particles

waste material is expelled

food vacuole

Putting It All Together

How do all the parts of the cell fit together? Think of a cell as a restaurant. The membrane is the door. The nucleus is the restaurant manager who decides what the menu will be. The cytoplasm is like the kitchen. This is where the items on the menu are prepared. Inside the kitchen, the mitochondria are the ovens. They provide the energy needed for the work to be done.

The ER are the cooks who prepare the dishes. Then the Golgi apparatus is the head waiter who packages the meals for delivery. It makes sure every dish goes to the proper customer. Meanwhile, lysosomes serve as the restaurant's recycling bin. And vacuoles are the cupboards that store supplies for another day.

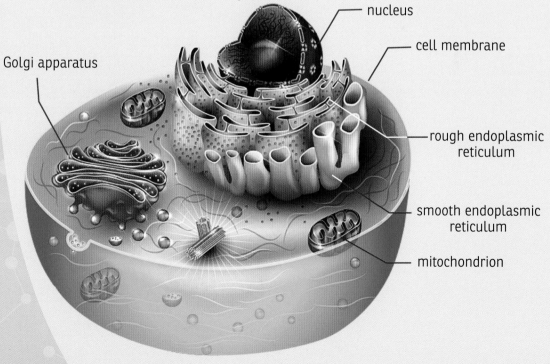

nucleus

cell membrane

Golgi apparatus

rough endoplasmic reticulum

smooth endoplasmic reticulum

mitochondrion

CHAPTER 4

Cell Division

There are two different kinds of cell division — mitosis and meiosis. Mitosis and meiosis work together and depend on each other. Mitosis helps living things grow new cells and repair damaged cells. Meiosis allows them to produce new offspring.

Mitosis

Every time a body cell divides, it creates two copies of itself. This is called mitosis.

Cell division is how animals grow. No matter how huge animals may be, they all begin as a single cell. The cell splits in half to form two cells, and the two cells split again. The cells keep dividing. Soon these cells are able to communicate with each other. They form groups that take on their own jobs. Some of these groups become bone cells or skin cells. Other groups include muscle, blood, or nerve cells.

PHASES OF MITOSIS

Mitosis has four main phases: prophase, metaphase, anaphase, and telophase.

Before mitosis, cells are in interphase. This is an in-between time when cells carry out their everyday jobs. A cell spends most of its time in interphase. Near the end of interphase, the cell makes a copy of each DNA molecule. Now it has two copies of every strand of DNA.

Some cells make copies of themselves quickly. A sea urchin cell takes about two hours to duplicate. Others take longer. It takes about 22 hours for a human liver cell to copy itself.

Every day millions of dead cells rub off a person's skin. Yet the skin does not show wear and tear from day to day. What is happening? New skin cells are replacing the ones that have been lost. These new cells are also created during the process of mitosis.

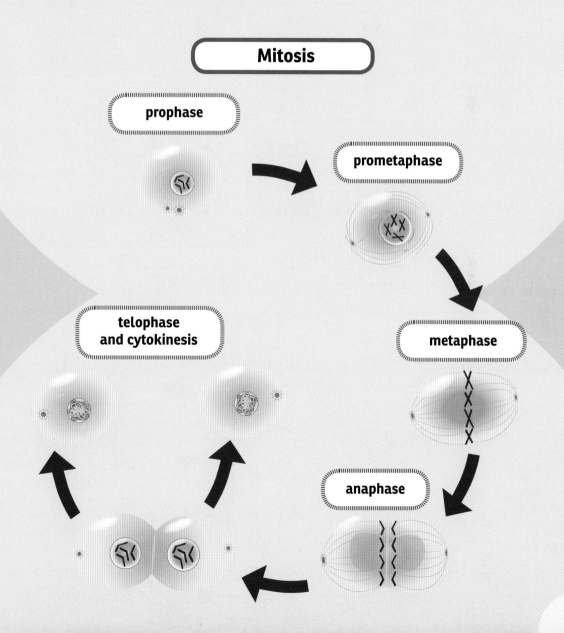

Mitosis

prophase

prometaphase

metaphase

anaphase

telophase
and cytokinesis

Meiosis

The second kind of cell division is called meiosis. This process makes sex cells. Meiosis does not make exact copies of genomes. It shuffles genes around. It creates cells that have half the number of chromosomes of body cells.

Meiosis makes egg cells in female animals and sperm cells in male animals. Meiosis produces four cells from one parent cell. These cells are called **gametes**. Each daughter cell contains half of the DNA from the parent cell.

Meiosis happens in two stages, and each stage has four main phases. They have the same names as the stages in mitosis: prophase, metaphase, anaphase, and telophase.

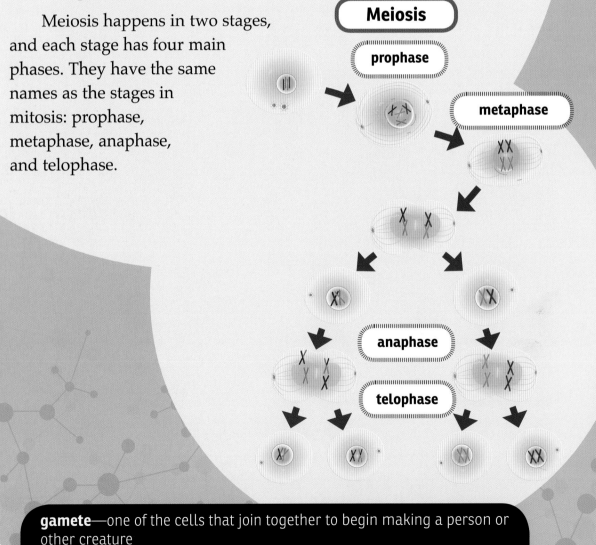

Meiosis

prophase

metaphase

anaphase

telophase

gamete—one of the cells that join together to begin making a person or other creature

One in every 691 babies is born with Down syndrome.

FACT

The second stage of meiosis is called meiosis II. Meiosis II is similar to mitosis, but there is no interphase. The cell does not make copies of the chromosomes.

MUTATIONS

Sometimes cells make mistakes when copying DNA. Cells usually detect and fix these errors, but sometimes they don't. These mistakes are mutations. Chemicals or radiation can sometimes cause mutations. Some mutations are just random accidents.

Mutations can be harmful. Too much sunlight can cause mutations in skin cells. These mutations may lead to cancer.

Some inherited diseases found in humans are caused by the mutation of a single gene. Sickle cell disease and Tay-Sachs disease are examples of single-gene mutations.

Humans can end up with too many chromosomes. Others can have too few. Down syndrome is a genetic disorder in which people have an extra chromosome in one of the chromosome pairs.

Most mutations have no effect, and some are helpful. Some mutations happen during meiosis and can be passed from one generation to the next. Over time, these mutations can even create new species.

CHAPTER 5

Animal Cell Types

An animal's body has many kinds of cells. Each one has a special job to do. To do their jobs, the various kinds of cells use their parts differently.

Red and white blood cells flow through veins.

Blood Cells

There are two kinds of blood cells, red and white. **Red blood cells** carry oxygen from the lungs to all the cells of the body. They also carry carbon dioxide away from the cells and to the lungs to breathe out. **White blood cells** fight disease.

A mature red blood cell is the only kind of cell that does not have a nucleus. A red blood cell is mainly made of the protein **hemoglobin**. This protein plays an important role in breathing. It picks up oxygen from the lungs and carries it through blood vessels to the cells.

To flow easily through blood vessels, red blood cells are round and smooth. They are shaped like flattened disks. A red blood cell is very flexible too. It can squeeze through even the smallest blood vessels.

White blood cells have special detectors on their membranes to find foreign invaders. Several kinds of white blood cells work together to fight germs. Some send out an alarm when they spot invaders. Others give off toxins that kill germs. Several white blood cells kill by surrounding germs, swallowing them up, and dissolving them.

Red blood cells are shaped like discs. White blood cells have an irregular shape.

red blood cell—a cell in the blood that carries oxygen from the lungs to all the tissues and cells of the body

white blood cell—a colorless blood cell that helps to protect the body against infections

hemoglobin—a substance in red blood cells that carries oxygen and gives blood its red color

Muscle Cells

Skeletal muscles connect bones. They move arms and legs, make tails swish, and help animals bite and chew. Muscle cells are long and thin. Under a microscope these cells look like they have light and dark bands. The bands are really strands of two different proteins. These protein strands move past each other and cause muscles to contract or relax. A single muscle cell has hundreds of mitochondria. Those organelles convert all the energy that muscles need to work.

Skeletal muscle can be found along bones in the arms.

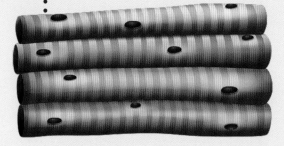

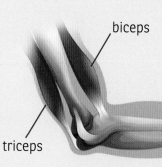

biceps

triceps

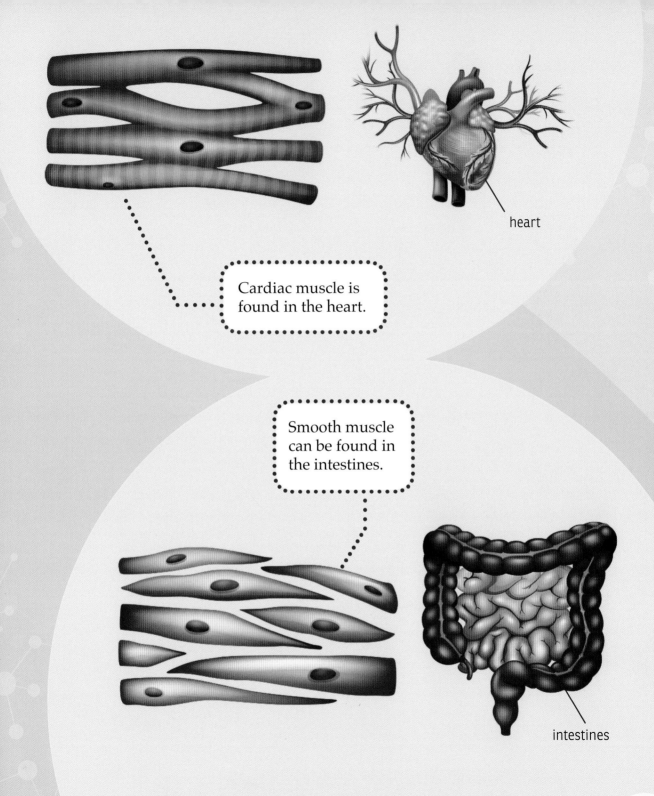

Cardiac muscle is found in the heart.

heart

Smooth muscle can be found in the intestines.

intestines

Nerve Cells

Animals can feel, taste, smell, touch, hear, and see because of nerve cells. Nerve cells, called **neurons**, also trigger muscles, including the heart. Nerve cells do all this by passing along messages to and from the brain.

A nerve cell looks like an octopus with long arms that reach out from a bulge in the center. The center, or cell body, processes signals coming into and going out of the cell. The "arms" are axons and dendrites that reach out to other neurons.

neurons and the nervous system

neuron—a nerve cell that is the basic working unit of the nervous system

dendrites

cell body

Neurons use over 50 types of neurotransmitters to communicate with each other.

direction of nerve impulse

axon

Many nerve cells have one axon and several dendrites. The dendrites pick up incoming signals. The axon passes along signals going out to the next cell. Many neurons bundle together to form a large network that carries messages to and from the brain. The longest cells in human bodies are sensory neurons that run from the bottom of their brain to their toes.

synapse

Skin Cells

Skin cells protect all other cells inside an animal's body. In humans the top part of the skin is called the epidermis. It is a thin sheet that covers most of the body. The epidermis is made up of several layers of skin cells. Each layer has a different job to do.

Skin cells in the outer layer are dead. These cells make the skin waterproof because they contain a tough protein called keratin. Dead skin cells wash off easily.

Skin cells in the middle layers make the keratin that is so important in the outer layer. In the bottom layer, new skin cells are always forming. They will move up to the top layer, die, and rub off. Some cells in the bottom layer also make a protein called melanin. Melanin gives skin its color and protects it from the sun's harmful rays.

FACT

Humans naturally and constantly lose skin cells. Millions of skin cells are shed every day.

Structure of the Epidermis

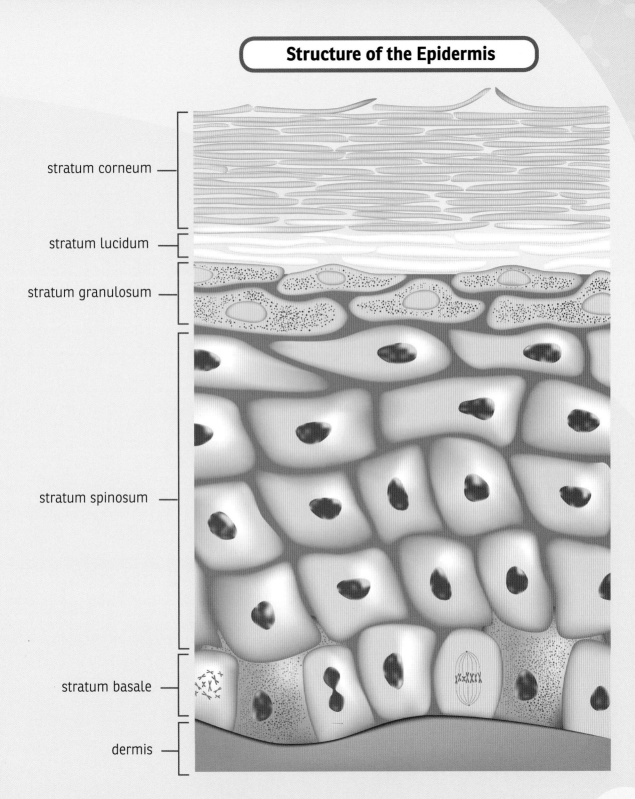

stratum corneum

stratum lucidum

stratum granulosum

stratum spinosum

stratum basale

dermis

29

Glossary

chromosome (KROH-muh-sohm)—threadlike structure in the nucleus that carries the genes

deoxyribonucleic acid (DNA) (DE-awk-see-ri-boh-new-klee-ik a-SUHD)—the molecule that carries the genes; found inside the nucleus of cells

gamete (GAM-et)—one of the cells that join together to begin making a person or other creature

gene (JEEN)—tiny unit of a cell that determines the characteristics that an offspring gets from his or her parents

hemoglobin (HEE-muh-gloh-bin)—a substance in red blood cells that carries oxygen and gives blood its red color

neuron (NOO-rahn)—a nerve cell that is the basic working unit of the nervous system

organelle (or-guh-NELL)—a small structure in a cell that performs a specific function and is surrounded by its own membrane

red blood cell (RED bluhd sel)—a cell in the blood that carries oxygen from the lungs to all the tissues and cells of the body

ribonucleic acid (RNA) (RI-boh-new-klee-ik a-SUHD)—the complex molecule produced by living cells and viruses that is responsible for manufacturing the protein in a cell

white blood cell (WITE-bluhd sel)—a colorless blood cell that helps to protect the body against infections

Read More

Duke, Shirley. *Cells*. The Science of Life. Minneapolis: ABDO Publishing Company, 2014.

Garbe, Suzanne. *Living Earth: Exploring Life on Earth with Science Projects*. Discover Earth Science. North Mankato, Minn.: Capstone Press, 2016.

Nelson, Maria. *Cells Up Close*. Under the Microscope. New York: Gareth Stevens Publishing, 2014.

Internet Sites

FactHound offers a safe, fun way to find Internet sites related to this book. All of the sites on FactHound have been researched by our staff.

Here's all you do:

Visit *www.facthound.com*

Type in this code: 9781515772590

Super-cool stuff! Check out projects, games and lots more at **www.capstonekids.com**

Critical Thinking Questions

- Identify two animal cell organelles from the diagram on page 17. What are their purposes?

- DNA stands for deoxyribonucleic acid. What is DNA?

- What are the three main parts of an animal cell?

Index